Affirmations for young Muslims to promote positivity, confidence, and a strong connection with their faith.

I am proud of my identity as a Muslim, embracing the diversity within the Ummah and showing respect to all.

I am an ambassador of peace, spreading love, tolerance, and respect, embodying the true spirit of Islam.

I am never alone, Allah is always near.

[Allah] said, "Fear not. Indeed, I am with you both; I hear and I see. (The Holy Quran 20:46)

I find strength in my daily prayers and connect with Allah through sincere worship.

I can talk to Allah about anything.

And your Lord said, 'Call on Me, I will respond to you.'"

(The Holy Quran 40:60)

I seek forgiveness for my mistakes and aim to improve myself with Allah's guidance.

I am grateful for the blessings and challenges in my life, as they are all from Allah's wisdom and mercy.

I am kind and compassionate towards others, following the teachings of Prophet Muhammad (peace be upon him.)

I am grateful for the opportunities I have to help those in need, following the teachings of charity in Islam.

I have faith in Allah's plan for me and trust that everything will unfold according to His will.

"And it may be that you dislike a thing which is good for you and that you like a thing which is bad for you. Allah knows but you do not know."
(The Holy Quran 2:216)

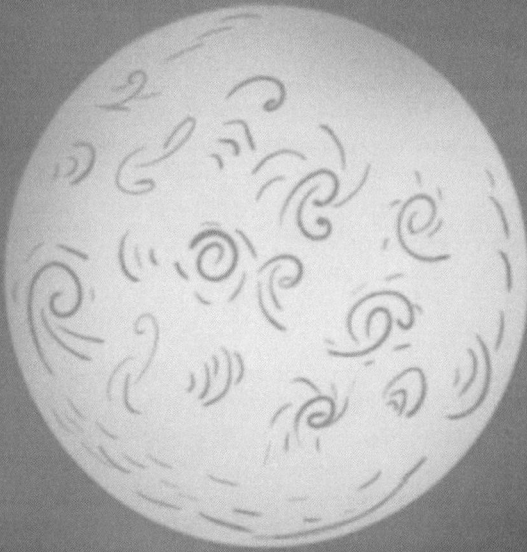

A.meen.

ISBN: 978-0-6455554-4-8
First Printed in 2023.
©Copyright 1000 Tales.

Written and Illustrated by
Ameera Karimshah

We would like to acknowledge the Traditional Custodians of the continent of Australia. Whose cultures are among the oldest living cultures in human history and whose languages and knowledge have infused and inhabited this land for millennia.

We recognise their continuing connection to the land, waters and culture and we pay our respects to their Elders past, present and emerging

* 9 7 8 0 6 4 5 5 5 5 4 4 8 *